CA$H IN ON
YOUR SKILLS

WAYS TO
MAKE MONEY WORKING
WITH KIDS

ALEXANDRA TRITTO

Enslow Publishing
101 W. 23rd Street
Suite 240
New York, NY 10011
USA
enslow.com

Published in 2020 by Enslow Publishing, LLC
101 W. 23rd Street, Suite 240, New York, NY 10011

Cataloging-in-Publication Data

Names: Tritto, Alexandra.
Title: Ways to make money working with kids / Alexandra Tritto.
Description: New York : Enslow Publishing, 2020. | Series: Cash in on your skills | Includes glossary and index.
Identifiers: ISBN 9781978515543 (pbk.) | ISBN 9781978515550 (library bound)
Subjects: LCSH: Child care—Vocational guidance—Juvenile literature. | Teaching—Vocational guidance—Juvenile literature. | Money-making projects for children—Juvenile literature.
Classification: LCC HQ778.5 T758 2020 | DDC 649'.023'73—dc23

Printed in China

To Our Readers: We have done our best to make sure all websites in this book were active and appropriate when we went to press. However, the author and the publisher have no control over and assume no liability for the material available on those websites or on any websites they may link to. Any comments or suggestions can be sent by email to customerservice@enslow.com.

Portions of this book originally appeared in *Money-Making Opportunities for Teens Who Like Working With Kids* by Susan Henneberg.

Photo Credits: Cover granata68/Shutterstock.com; p. 5 Khosrork/iStock/Getty Images; p. 9 wavebreakmedia/Shutterstock.com; p. 10 Ashwin/Shutterstock.com; p. 12 Dmytro Zinkevych/Shutterstock.com; pp. 14, 62 Monkey Business Images /Shutterstock.com; p. 17 carballo/Shutterstock.com; p. 20 Rawpixel.com/Shutterstock .com; p. 23 Deanna Kelly/Moment/Getty Images; p. 26 bibiphoto/Shutterstock.com; p. 30 skynesher/E+/Getty Images; p. 33 Selenophile/Shutterstock.com; p. 35 Red Chopsticks/Getty Images; p. 38 West Rock/The Image Bank/Getty Images; p. 40 AAresTT/Shutterstock.com; p. 42 Africa Studio/Shutterstock.com; p. 48 kenary820 /Shutterstock.com; p. 50 pickingpok/Shutterstock.com; p. 53 AndreyPopov /iStock/Getty Images; p. 55 serdjophoto/Shutterstock.com; p. 61 Hill Street Studios /DigitalVision/Getty Images; pp. 66, 68 sturti/E+/Getty Images.

CONTENTS

Finding a babysitter can be difficult. An even bigger challenge? Finding a *good* babysitter. After all, playing together sounds a lot more fun than watching someone be on his or her phone the entire time. That's why Noa Mintz decided to start her own business, Nannies by Noa, when she was just twelve years old. In an interview with *Entrepreneur*, Noa said she was frustrated with several nannies as they "stood off to the sidelines on playgrounds, fumbling with their cell phones."

Noa founded Nannies by Noa in an effort to recruit better babysitters. What started as a small side gig has turned into a huge success. With over 190 clients and a thorough application process to find the best babysitters around, Noa, who is now a student at Brown University, has even had to hire a CEO to help her run the business!

Noa saw a problem—disengaged babysitters—and thought of a solution, which she then turned into a business. Whether it's working with children directly or creating a business of your own, you, too, can work hard and make some money. There are many opportunities for teens to work with children, and even better, these jobs can be extremely fulfilling, interesting, and fun.

People who work with children often build close relationships with them, something many teens find particularly meaningful.

In addition to babysitting, many summer camps and after-school programs are always looking for caring, attentive teens to be counselors for the younger children. In these positions, employees are expected to be there not just for the money but also because they want to help and mentor the kids around them. There may be several different opportunities within summer camps and after-school programs. For example, camps might be hiring an arts and crafts counselor, a lifeguard, or a sports coach. Similarly, schools may also offer a range of after-school programs focused on different subjects or activities. When thinking about which opening to apply for, it's important to consider your own interests and goals. While it is work and requires you to be responsible, this can be something you enjoy, too!

Tutoring is another great way to earn money. Many children, and their parents, seek help from older kids to better their knowledge in a subject or two, so teaching jobs can be found all over. These openings may be posted in schools, on the internet, in your local community center, or spread by word of mouth. In addition, there are things you can do to advertise your skills and services, like hanging posters where allowed.

All of these jobs, as well as many others, will give you a great deal of experience all while earning some extra cash. As you continue to grow older, it's important to be on the lookout for opportunities around you. The knowledge and skills you continue to learn will help you tremendously in furthering your education and career. And even if you decide that working with children isn't for you, that's okay, too. All of your experiences together can be used to help you follow whatever path you take. A lot of them, like good communication, will translate into other areas of your life. Of course, earning an income is great, but it's important to keep in mind that you'll also be gaining something else: knowledge.

Getting Started

Are you interested in working with children? If so, welcome to the club! There are many people who work with kids, as well as many types of jobs that allow you to work with children. In 2018, public schools in the United States alone employed approximately 3.2 million full-time teachers. Add that number to people who teach at other places, such as private institutions or universities, and that number becomes even higher. And, of course, teaching isn't the only way you can work with kids. The possibilities are endless!

Working with children requires enthusiasm and eagerness. When thinking about what types of jobs you might be interested in, it is important to be honest with yourself. What are you excited about? What do you enjoy? What skills do you want to put to use and continue to develop? Lots of people may love children but find that they don't enjoy working with them professionally.

It's no secret that work is work. There will probably be times when you are stressed, busy,

Identifying your own interests is a good place to start when thinking about what subject you'd like to teach.

anxious, or confused—all of which are normal feelings to experience—but keep in mind that your career should be in a field that you are passionate about. While it may at times be hard, work should ultimately be rewarding and interesting. And remember: When something is challenging, you usually grow as a person as a result.

How Working for Kids Works for You

There are many benefits to working besides the money. Learning new skills can help teenagers discover what their interests and passions are and help them find jobs in the future. For some, working is the first time they gain exposure to finances and money management. They gain experience in dealing with stress and conflict. They learn to interact with a variety of people and different personalities. They also gain confidence as they take on more adult-like responsibilities.

Parents and employers benefit as well. Teens usually work for less money than adults. They tend to engage with children easily. Even in positions of authority, teens are often able to

It can take some time to adjust to a new job, so remember to be patient with yourself.

relate to kids, breaking down some age barriers that allow for a more understanding relationship.

We or Me?

There are many positions, environments, and ways in which you can work with kids. First, you should think about if you want to work for someone else, like an established business or organization. For instance, you might enjoy supervising kids in an after-school program. The advantages to working for someone else include having a standard schedule and dependable paycheck. However, there are disadvantages as well. Your job might have little variety and become predictable. As a teenager, your pay is unlikely to surpass minimum wage.

Other teens might want to work for themselves and start their own businesses. For example, you might tutor kids in math or teach guitar lessons. The advantage to this approach is that you are in control. You make your own schedule, so you can work as much or as little as you want. You're also the one who decides what to charge clients for your services. However, there are many challenges to becoming an entrepreneur. You will have to promote your services to get clients. There might be slow times when you make little money or, on

People who have started their own businesses are known as entrepreneurs.

the contrary, there might be stressful times when too many things are happening at once. To be a successful business owner, you need excitement, organization, and good money-management skills.

SOME POINTERS FOR WORKING WITH KIDS

- Get to know the children you're working with. All of us want to be seen as individuals, not just part of a group. Take the time to ask kids questions about themselves and see if there's anything you have in common, like owning a pet.

- Keep directions simple and positive. No one likes being told what to do. Children are less likely to cooperate when given negative instructions, like "Don't run in the hallways." Instead, try something more positive, like "Walk inside."

- Be calm and levelheaded when approaching conflict and discipline. When someone begins to argue with you, it's natural to want to argue back. However, this isn't productive and only causes things to escalate. Rather, tell the children what you need them to do and what will happen if they don't do it. Follow through with the consequences if appropriate. This way, the children will know what's expected of them.

Open Mind, Open Heart

When working with others, it's crucial to remember the importance of respect. You may encounter children who come from families and homes very similar to yours. You may meet children who do the same things you did as a kid, making it easy for you to relate to their experiences. However, chances are

Working is a great way to meet new people, especially those with similar career interests as you.

you will also work with some children who are very different from you, be it race, gender, socioeconomic status, sexuality, ability, or something else. Working with children requires you to be aware of these differences without treating anyone as an outsider.

This awareness needs to be handled with an open mind. Remember that you can't judge a book by its cover. While some things may be obvious, such as a wheelchair needed for mobility assistance, many things are not. While a wheelchair is visible, a learning disability, for example, is not. For these reasons and more, it is key that you treat all children with dignity and respect. An inclusive environment is a win-win for all.

Finding a Job

A t the beginning, finding a job can seem daunting. You may not know where to start or what to do. Fortunately, there are plenty of resources available at your disposal. Before diving into your research and applications, though, it's a good idea to talk to a parent or guardian. You may be itching to take the first steps toward finding a job and excited to make some money, but a job is a big responsibility. It's a decision you should think through and run by your parents to get their thoughts, too. Consider your schedule, for example. Does your weekly routine allow time for a job? If not, you may have to give up an extracurricular activity to make sure you're available to work.

Most employers require their employees to work a minimum number of hours. Although this number is typically lower for minors than adults, you need to be able to promise your boss that you can dedicate the time needed for the job. You should also think of yourself. If you have a lot on your plate, it may not be the best time to take on a job. Morten Hansen, a professor at University of California, Berkeley,

Good time-management skills are essential when you have a job. For some, planners or calendar apps are helpful organization tools.

and author of *Great at Work*, says that we should all work with the goal to "do less, then obsess." After studying over 5,000 managers and employees, he found that people perform better when they take on a smaller set of tasks that they're able to prioritize and focus on. By contrast, employees who take on more work have a much harder time excelling. They spread themselves too thin and find it difficult to juggle all of their projects. Accepting a job when it's not appropriate for you, or taking on too many jobs, is unfair to both you and your employer.

Where to Start

It hasn't been that long since you were a kid, right? When looking for a job, think back to the places where you enjoyed spending time when you were younger. These might be the perfect places for you to consider working. Before you begin applying, make sure you have all the tools you need to conduct a productive job search. Here are some steps to take:

1. **Prepare a résumé and cover letter.** Your résumé should be no longer than one page and should be tailored to the jobs you're applying to. You don't need a different résumé for each job application, but it's a good idea to list all of your experience relevant to children when applying for a job that involves working with them. Your cover letter should also only be a page long, but unlike your résumé, you should write a different one for each job you apply to. You can start with a template, but make sure that your cover letter is specific to the position and company you're applying to!

2. **Google yourself.** It's not uncommon for employers to search their candidates online. They want to make sure there are no red flags before hiring someone. They may use your social media content to evaluate your character and personality. The last thing they want to see are inappropriate photos or posts. A 2018 CareerBuilder survey reported that 70 percent of employers use social media to assess job applicants and 43 percent of employers use social media to check up on current employees! Keep in mind that once you land a job, you will be representing the company—or family—you work for. An employee's social media image can reflect badly on your employer at large.

3. **Utilize your resources.** We don't always see what's right in front of us. While the internet can be a great place to find job openings, there might be someone you know who could use some help. Maybe your mom's friend needs a babysitter or the summer camp you went to as a kid is hiring. Whatever the circumstances are, it's smart to check in with those around you and see if they know of any available positions.

Teaching Toddlers

If you're interested in working with toddlers and young children, daycare centers and preschools are good places to start. Some of these are franchises of large corporations, and some are small businesses run by local entrepreneurs. Others are nonprofits organized by local governments or religious institutions.

The age at which kids must start school varies by state, ranging from five to eight years old.

Many states require daycare and teacher assistants to be at least eighteen years old. However, some states have lowered this age to sixteen. Most schools ask employees to get trained in basic first aid and cardiopulmonary resuscitation (CPR). All states mandate that applicants go through pre-hire background checks. The majority of daycares are not open on weekends, so all shifts are assigned on weekdays. Still, daycare centers often offer different time slots, so there is usually some flexibility in the schedule, allowing you to work after school.

So Many Choices

Working with older children is another intriguing and fun option. Local elementary schools are frequently hiring teenagers to run or assist with their after-school programs. These programs offer supervision for children while parents are at work. Your duties might include preparing snacks, helping with homework, and organizing and leading games or crafts. These kinds of jobs will likely fit well with your school schedule.

Another school-related job is tutoring. Tutoring is a great way to use your knowledge in a subject to help someone else. Not only will your student be learning, but you'll also get the chance to practice whatever subject you love! There are a couple of different ways to find tutoring jobs. There may be some local tutoring businesses in your community looking for teenagers to help children with math, writing, and reading comprehension. In this setting, you'll usually have individual sessions with your student at the tutoring center. Another option is to look online and see if anyone in your neighborhood is hiring a tutor. Care.com is a great website that allows you to filter your job search based on your zip code and connect with people via private messages. Whenever using a site like that, use your best judgment and be cautious about giving out personal information. Make sure an adult in your life knows about the online chat. You may also want to reach out to your own school staff and ask if they have any opportunities.

There are many places to consider applying for a job if you are athletic. Some of these include dance studios, ice skating rinks, tennis clubs, and swimming pools. You might be able to teach lessons at these venues or you might supervise open play. Sometimes certifications are needed. For example, lifeguards and swim instructors need to pass a Red Cross lifeguard or water safety instructor course.

Some places might prefer teens that have successfully competed at a high level. Whatever

A Red Cross lifeguard certificate is valid for two years. Lifeguards must get recertified once that time is up.

your experience level is, many teen athletes enjoy being able to pass on their skills to younger sports enthusiasts.

Other jobs to consider may be at zoos, museums, and camps. For example, many larger communities have art, history, or science museums. There are even some museums specifically for children, like the Children's Museum of Manhattan. Other institutions cater to all ages but have a children's section or special activities to engage kids in their exhibits. Working teens might find themselves demonstrating electricity, showing off baby animals, or supervising a historical dress-up activity. Day and overnight summer camps often hire teen counselors. They usually prefer teens that have camp experience. Counselors may need to be competent in swimming, horseback riding, crafts, or other activities.

Finally, water parks and amusement parks are found in many communities. They rely on teens to cope with the many children who fill them each summer. Patience and the ability to remain calm under pressure are important traits for teens who apply for these jobs.

The Small Things Aren't So Small

It's not just the work itself that's hard. There can be many other challenges, like getting to and from your job and figuring out what to wear. It can also be difficult to maintain a positive attitude when you are tired or stressed.

A reliable mode of transportation is really important. Your employer will expect you to get to work on time, so take transportation into account when accepting a job. A nearby job that pays less

PRACTICING BALANCE

Working a paid job will definitely increase your bank account. However, you need to consider the trade-offs that come with having a job and how you'll balance your time. With a new job, you will probably find yourself busier than before. You will have less free time to spend with friends and family, do schoolwork, and relax. You have to think about how you'll manage your time wisely. You will also need to identify your priorities and decide when to say no. Unfortunately, it's impossible to do everything. With the responsibility of having a job comes the responsibility of learning to balance your life, too.

might be a better choice than one farther away and is difficult to get to. Take advantage of any carpooling you can do with coworkers. You will need to subtract the costs of public transportation, gas, or parking from the money you make at your job. It's helpful to know the best route and how long your commute usually takes. Using this information, you can decide on a set time to leave for work. There may be a time when you're late to work because of something out of your control, say an accident held up traffic or all trains were delayed due to bad weather. In these

In some states, public transportation is more expensive during rush hour. These elevated prices are often referred to as peak fares.

situations, try to get in contact with your employer and explain why you're running late.

Teen workers may be required to wear a uniform. Even if you don't love the outfit, make an effort to keep it looking neat and clean. Wrinkled or stained clothing sends a message that you don't care about your job. If you have choices about what to wear, take cues from your supervisors and coworkers about what is appropriate. If you have a hard time telling what the dress code expectations are, don't be afraid to ask. When working with kids, you want to wear comfortable but professional clothing that allows you to move. You should also take into account the weather and what you'll be doing. You don't want to be wearing pants and a long-sleeved shirt on the hottest day of the year, and you certainly don't want to be wearing flip-flops for a hike. Remember, when you are on the job, you represent your employer.

Even more important than your attire is your attitude. Your employer expects you to arrive on time, energized, enthusiastic, and positive. There is no room in the workplace for gossip or drama. If you encounter a problem, follow the protocol to get it resolved as quickly and as efficiently as possible. These behaviors will be recognized and rewarded. Your employer will also appreciate professional behavior with regard to your cell phone use. While you may be asked to carry a phone for the safety of the children you're supervising, be responsible. Save checking your text messages for your breaks.

When joining the workforce, most people start from the bottom and climb their way up. Entry-level positions are a great way to learn how to be an employee. Teens who work hard and maintain a good attitude can quickly move into more responsible positions.

Getting Down to Business

Working with kids is often centered, in one way or another, on fun and entertainment. Teens who babysit, throw birthday parties, and serve as camp counselors are always thinking up new fun activities and making sure their kids are having a good time.

Even children-related jobs that are more behind the scenes do this. Think about the managers of children's museums as an example. They may not spend as much time working directly with kids compared to a tour leader, but it's the manager who coordinates all of the exhibits, makes sure things are running smoothly, and oversees the museum that provides children with a fun place to visit in the first place. That's not to say one position is more important than another. At any job, all employees should be valued—no matter their status.

Babysitting and Beyond

There are many different types of businesses that involve working with kids. Today's busy parents are grateful to find teens who can babysit, host a playgroup, or organize a birthday party. Teens can also give lessons or tutor a difficult subject.

Babysitting is a natural business for teens. Teenagers are generally available after school and in the evenings when parents need them. There are also opportunities to babysit on weekends. In this way, babysitting is often a good match for a teen's schedule. The Red Cross offers babysitting and first aid classes. Getting certificates in these classes will give you—and parents—the confidence that you can handle emergencies.

A similar business is a weekly after-school or weekend playgroup. Many parents would appreciate some time to themselves while taking comfort knowing that their children are safe and having fun. This is a good business to run with a friend so you have someone to share the tasks and responsibilities with. You need to have a good head for organization. It also takes some investment in supplies. You can organize a theme for each week. Offer games, activities both inside and outside, crafts, and a snack.

Playgroups can also be structured based on interests and ages. For example, you could run an arts and crafts playgroup or a toddlers-only playgroup.

You should speak with your parents to figure out how many children you can accommodate at one time. State regulations vary, but most allow teens to care for children in their homes without a license or insurance as long as it is for less than three hours a day.

Teens skilled in music or a sport might consider giving lessons. Other teens may give lessons in

SAFETY FIRST

Safety, both your own and that of the children under your care, must always be a primary concern. You should never put yourself in a situation that would make you or your clients uncomfortable. Here are some good safety tips:

- Create an information form for each child under your care. Ask parents or guardians if the child has any health issues, such as asthma or allergies.
- Make sure you have several emergency phone numbers to call for each child.
- If you are taking the children anywhere besides your home, get permission forms signed by their parents.

Being prepared for any emergencies will give you and the parents that entrust you with their children some peace of mind.

cheerleading and hip-hop dancing. There are many other skills and talents teens have to offer younger kids. Busy parents might love to have their children learn such skills as cooking, sewing, or crochet. Elementary or middle school kids are not too young to learn the basics of jewelry making, bicycle repair, or web design from a patient teen with solid abilities.

Another moneymaking service is tutoring. According to an interview in *Dallas News*, Guatam Bhargava founded a whole tutoring company called Peeyr! Peeyr offers tutoring sessions in all subjects and across all grade levels. The tutors are high school and college students. While the company is focused on traditional educational subjects, Bhargava plans to incorporate things that cater to children's interests, like hosting chess lessons.

Why a Business Plan Matters

A business plan is like a road map. It is a written plan to help you figure out where you are going in your business and how you will get there. Your business plan should include a short paragraph describing what your business actually is.

Describing your business may sound really easy, but it can sometimes be difficult to put into words. A business plan is also helpful for showing adults that you know what you are doing. A business plan details what services the business will offer and what money and resources it will require.

Some businesses don't cost much to run. For example, babysitting only requires transportation to the job, though some babysitters might choose to invest in some games or DVDs. Tutoring may require educational materials such as workbooks and other

As your business evolves, so, too, will your business plan. Remember to look at your business plan every once in a while so you can make any necessary changes.

school supplies. For cooking classes, you usually need to put money into equipment and materials. To estimate the costs of running a business, you will need to distinguish between fixed costs and variable costs. For example, for cooking lessons, buying a set of pots and pans is a one-time, fixed cost. Buying ingredients for different recipes each week, on the other hand, is a variable cost since the prices will change based on what you're making.

Developing a Business Plan

Follow these steps to create a strong business plan. This way, you will have everything you need to start and grow your business.

The first step when drafting your business plan is to describe your business idea and your goals. Your plan should explain what services you will provide. It can also be a good idea to describe your competition. What similar businesses exist in your community? What can you provide that they cannot? If there is a lot of competition, you may have to narrow down and find a specialty for your business. For instance, if many people offer birthday parties, you might specialize in popular princess parties for little girls. This is a good way to distinguish yourself and make your business unique and memorable.

Deciding how to price your services will take some research. You can use the internet to see what competitors charge for similar work or you can call local companies and ask for their price list. You can try to undercut them, or price your services significantly lower than theirs, to steer customers your way. Charging less for a similar service, however, will impact your earnings. Instead, think of ways you can provide extra value. For example, there may be many bright teens available to tutor middle school students in algebra. To stand out, you might advertise that you can throw in some standardized test prep for free.

Also describe how you plan to market your business. How will customers find out about your services? One way is to post flyers and hand out business cards. There are resources in most word-processing programs to help you design these promotional items. Post your flyers where potential customers might see them. Many local cafés, gyms, and grocery stores have community bulletin boards. You can also create business cards to hand out to potential clients. You might even create your own website.

Keeping good financial records is very important in a business. The Small Business Administration (SBA) suggests that you begin by creating a start-up budget. This lists the costs of equipment and supplies

Make sure your numbers are accurate. Research the prices and costs that will influence your budget so you can plan appropriately.

you need to begin your business, as well as other business-related costs. For example, you might need to pay for a CPR class for some babysitting positions. Remember to factor in how much these things will cost and how you will get this money.

You will also need to create an operating budget. An operating budget tracks operating expenses and profits and losses. This information is often organized on a spreadsheet. Using your operating budget, you can determine how much money you are making—or losing—at any given time.

You need to save all the receipts for items you buy for your business. The costs of these items are considered business expenses. The receipts will be necessary for tax forms.

Similarly, it is also important to give your customers receipts for their purchases. A simple way to do this is to buy a receipt book from an office supply store. These are duplicate forms. When you fill out a receipt for the customer, there will be a copy behind for you to keep for your records.

Putting together a business plan may seem complicated and time-consuming. However, the time you spend organizing your business will pay off. Knowing exactly what your goals are and what you need to achieve them will save you time and money as you continue to develop your business. These organizational skills will also contribute to your success in the future.

Get Creative

Most successful companies have a logo, slogan, or both that make their businesses easy to recognize. Think of Nike's signature check mark or the yellow arches that McDonalds has. You, too, can design a logo or think up a slogan to put on business cards, flyers, and even clothing. This is a great way to advertise your business. Try and see if you can come up with a catchy business name. Avoid long, confusing names that may mislead your customers. Have fun with it, but remember that you want the name of your business to convey your brand and services. For a princess party business, you might look online for an image of a crown or draw one yourself. Put it next to a name like "Fairytale Parties." Print it in a fancy font on iron-on transfer paper from an office supply store. Apply it to a T-shirt, and you have your business attire. You can also buy sheets of business cards and stationery to print on.

Go Time!

While some small businesses take off immediately, most need constant marketing to grow. You will need to promote your company to attract new clients. The target audience for your advertising will probably be parents. Your materials have to look professional and be error-free.

Word of mouth is an effective way to get new business. If your clients like your business, they will tell their friends, family, and coworkers. Make sure that you treat your clients politely at all times. Rachel Wood, a teen who co-wrote and published her own book on teen entrepreneurship, advises, "If you are competing with other teens, customers will want the most courteous person. Go the extra mile." She also suggests asking clients to evaluate your service. If they

Making flyers and posters doesn't have to be expensive. To save some money, try using some art supplies you already own.

like what you have done, ask if they would be willing to act as a reference for future clients. Website testimonials can also attract potential clients down the line. Providing excellent customer service is the key to expanding your business.

Although it may feel overwhelming, starting a business is not an impossible dream for a teen. Thousands do it every year with great success. With energy, information, and a solid business plan, you can make your dream a reality. You may make a little money for some fun summer activities. Or you may become the next new teen millionaire. Either way, you will come out ahead. You will have learned how to plan and organize, how to manage money and people, and how to create and build something of your own. These are all things you should be proud of! These skills will provide a foundation for success in the years to come.

More Than Money

Sometimes when people get a job, they get lost in the cash signs. It can be easy to get caught up in the money of it all, especially if you've never had an income of your own before. And money is important!

But there are other things that you will gain from working, too. There will be successes to be celebrated, moments to be proud of, and milestones to be acknowledged. Although these things may not carry monetary value, they do have an inherently powerful personal value. Over the course of your career, you will have achieved many things—don't forget to recognize them.

Earning your own money is exciting! But it's important to remember that money isn't the only way to measure success.

Helping Others

Many organizations and nonprofits welcome teens looking to volunteer their time to work with children. Although volunteers are generally unpaid positions, there are many advantages to volunteering. Sometimes, these opportunities are a better fit rather than working a job or starting a business. Volunteers can often choose their own work schedule. This is useful for busy students who have a difficult class load or a lot of extracurricular activities. Volunteers can also get fun and exciting positions. Many nonprofit organizations cannot afford to hire a lot of people, so they rely on volunteers to take on necessary jobs. For example, teens can volunteer at Volunteers for Outdoor Colorado (VOC) and help work on the state's sustainability mission. VOC also hosts a lot of events for families, so volunteers have opportunities to help out with those as well. Teens ages sixteen and up can volunteer at Mississippi Children's Museum and take children through the exhibits, play with them, and help make the museum a fun, interactive experience.

Many large organizations, such as hospitals, school districts, and museums, have coordinators who place volunteers. Teens might entertain children receiving treatments in pediatric wards of

Research has shown that volunteering helps people feel better both physically and mentally.

hospitals. They might coach disadvantaged children on a sports team. A camp for disabled children might need volunteer counselors to organize games and activities. A nearby elementary school might need teens to help second graders work on math puzzles. Reading to children at a library story hour is another volunteer possibility.

Volunteering is rewarding in many different ways. Leadership, problem solving, and interacting

A VOLUNTEERING ENTREPRENEUR

More and more companies are beginning to value corporate social responsibility (CSR). As businesses learn how important volunteering is to their employees, they may develop programs in an effort to meet their workers' needs. According to Cone Research, two-thirds of millennials won't even think about accepting a job if the company doesn't have strong CSR values. And almost 90 percent report better performance in offices high in CSR. This trend hasn't gone unnoticed. Some corporations not only encourage volunteering but reward it as well. Employees at Deloitte, an international accounting organization, are paid for each hour they participate in one of the company's volunteer programs and there's no limit on how many hours someone can volunteer.

with diverse populations are just some of the skills teens learn in volunteer positions. They gain maturity and the confidence to cope with new situations. Volunteering is a great way to learn about potential careers. Volunteering can also be rewarding internally; it feels nice to know that you did something to help someone else.

Debby Ryan, the star of Disney Channel's *Jessie*, says that volunteering is a cool thing for teens to do. "Discover what you care about, and look for opportunities in your neighborhood to get involved," she told *USA Weekend*. Disney's Friends for Change program encourages teens to become leaders and be a catalyst for change in their own communities.

Learning on the Job

An internship is a formal program in which students gain experience in a workplace. Internships can vary in length, but they are usually at least a month long. Some places pay their interns—typically a small amount—while others give them school credit. Teens who do an internship learn what it is like to be an employee in the real world. They usually receive a mentor who helps them learn what it's like to be in the workplace. Interns learn what habits and attitudes employers expect from their employees. They are able to make connections between what they are learning in school and the skills needed on the job. This can lead to more motivation and higher grades. Internships provide teens with great experience and are impressive on résumés and college applications.

Internships are a good way to build career-specific skills and learn about different jobs. For example, before you decide that a career teaching kindergarten is for you, you might want to spend a few weeks or months interning in a classroom with older students. You might find that while you love teaching, you're actually more interested in working with older kids. An internship is a great chance to try out a job and see what it's like.

Your school counseling office or career center is a good first stop to learn about internships. Many high schools will arrange internships for students. In some high schools, students are expected to complete an internship before graduation. Friends and relatives can also suggest internship possibilities. Books and websites about internships offer ideas and listings, too.

Consider opportunities that might help you figure out your interests and strengths. Interning with child and youth services in the military might bring out your desire to serve the nation. An internship working with kids at a community arts agency could show your creative side. In any setting, interns learn the importance of good communication and organizational skills. They learn how to act professionally, maintain a positive attitude, and cope with challenges in the workplace.

Kai Curtis, who interned at the International Trade Administration (ITA), found his internship to be extremely valuable. His supervisor, Jeff G. Hall, made clear that he, too, thought the internship programs were beneficial—and not just for the interns. In a 2016 *Washington Post* article, he said, "We don't look at these interns as being separate from the team, we look at them as being part of the team." Kai's internship really solidified his passion for joining the ITA after college.

During challenging economic times, it is sometimes difficult for teens to find a job or start a business. If this is the case for you, consider volunteering or interning. Time spent improving the lives of others and increasing your own employability is well worth it. You could find the passion that will drive your life for many years.

Finances

For some, finances can seem really overwhelming. This is particularly true for teens that haven't had much exposure to money or experience managing money. If your school offers business classes, that's a great place to start. You can also talk to an adult you trust and ask them any questions you may have. Understanding how money, banks, and taxes work is necessary for life. As a teenager looking for a job, you'll need to learn some of the fundamentals early on. Don't be afraid to ask questions or ask for clarification if you're having trouble understanding something. In fact, research has shown that people who are more vocal about money have healthier relationships and report better self-assurance.

Don't Lose Sight of Your Goals

You wouldn't start a race without knowing where the finish line was, would you? That's what it's like to save money without having some goals in place. It can be easy to spend money without giving it so

Some people organize their short- and long-term goals into separate savings accounts. This makes it easy to see how much money you have for your different goals.

much as a second thought—especially when having your own money is new to you. It's tempting to spend money at the mall, fast-food restaurants, and vending machines.

Be in control of your money by setting specific short- and long-term goals. Review them frequently so that you don't forget them, and remember to update or revise your goals as you see fit. Put a brightly colored list of your goals in your wallet or purse. That way, when you take out your money to buy something, you will be reminded that you are saving for your goals.

A good way to think about financial goals is to distinguish between wants and needs. Your wants may be things like the latest gadgets, fashion accessories, movie tickets, and video games. Wants might even include expensive things, such as a senior trip or a new snowboard. These are fun to have. There is nothing wrong with setting aside a certain amount of your earnings to buy these things. You might allot a certain percentage of your paycheck or profits to these wants. However, you need to make sure you can pay for your needs.

Your needs are priority items, like college tuition or car payments. You may also need to contribute toward family expenses. Saving money takes commitment, discipline, and the ability to delay gratification. Your bank account won't double overnight; saving money takes time.

Don't get discouraged by this. It's also important to remember that as you save, you'll also be spending. This means that even as your savings grow, you could see a temporary dip between the time

Even something as small as saving your spare change can make a big difference in the long run. You'd be surprised at how many coins some people carry around!

you make a car payment and your next paycheck. When your friends are planning a day of shopping, eating out, and seeing a movie, you will have to be strong when deciding to save that money instead. That being said, you can (and should!) still spend time with friends. Maybe you just decide to meet them for a bite to eat and skip out on the shopping and movie that day to save some cash. Reminding yourself about your long-term goals will pay off as your savings account continues to grow.

You need to be very specific about the money required to meet your needs. For example, you may decide you want to attend a nearby state college. According to the College Board in 2018, the average price of one year's tuition at a public, four-year state school is $9,410. Let's say your parents expect you to pay half that amount, or $4,705. If so, you would need to save about $392 each month for a year to meet the goal of paying for one year of college. You might also be saving for a car. Depending on the car you choose and your loan interest rate, monthly payments for a car can vary by hundreds of dollars. However, a large down payment can lower monthly costs significantly. You also need to factor in state registration fees and the cost of car insurance.

For many teens, an important goal is to contribute money to charity. Leanna Archer started her own hair products company when she was eleven. Leanna told *USA Today* that she puts half the earnings from her business into a college savings account. She puts another quarter back into the business. The last 25 percent is donated to a Haitian charity for earthquake relief. Some teens even start their own charities. *CNN Money* profiled Asya Gonzalez, who, at thirteen, began her own T-shirt company. She donates a portion of every shirt sold to She's Worth It!, a nonprofit organization she founded. The organization is dedicated to ending human trafficking and child sex slavery.

Graduating from the Piggy Bank

It can be tricky to navigate your finances for the first time. Learning as much as you can, though, is the only way you will be able to make the best and most educated decisions for yourself. An important first step in becoming financially responsible is setting up checking and savings accounts at a bank near your home.

A checking account allows you to deposit money and then pay bills with paper checks or online. Banks usually provide you with a debit card when you open a checking account. Your debit card will have a unique number associated with it and can be used to pay in person and online. This money will come out of your checking account. When you are working, it's a good idea to have your employer deposit your paycheck directly into your checking account. This is known as direct deposit. With this method, your paycheck is sent to your bank instead of handed or

In addition to saving paper, electronic checks are also believed to be a more secure form of payment. With direct deposit, there's no chance of somebody stealing your check or trying to cash it.

mailed to you. You get to skip the step of depositing your check, and your funds are available quickly. If you'd like, employers can still provide you with a check even if you're enrolled in direct deposit. This is not another paycheck; it's an inactive check that serves as a personal statement or record. These are often available online, too.

Teens younger than eighteen will need a parent or guardian to cosign a checking account. This means that your parent will have access to the account. Also keep in mind that the bank may charge fees for its checking account services. Before opening an account, you may want to speak with someone at the bank and ask what charges, if any, come with the account and any other questions you may have.

In addition to writing checks and paying bills online, you will likely want to withdraw cash using your bank's automated teller machine (ATM). You may pay a fee to withdraw money from other banks' ATMs, so be sure to use your bank's machines when you can. To access your account from the ATM, you will need to insert your debit card into the machine and enter a four-digit pin that you will set up when you receive the card.

Accurate record keeping is essential to make sure you have enough money to cover payments and withdrawals. It's important to keep track of all your deposits and withdrawals. You also need to record every check you write, and it's helpful to add any purchases made with your debit card to this list as well. The bank will give you a check register to carry around with you. At the end of each month, you will receive a statement that lists all of your deposits, checks, debit card payments, and ATM withdrawals.

If you lose your debit card, call your bank immediately to cancel the card. That way, no one will be able to access the money in your account.

Learning how to reconcile your checking account, which involves checking your own records against the bank's statements, is an important financial skill. A bank representative can show you how to do this. Today, many bank customers also keep track of their money online, rather than waiting for the bank to send monthly statements.

MEET THE IRS

When you begin a paid job, you will have to fill out an Internal Revenue Service (IRS) form called a W-4. This form tells your employer how much money to withhold from your paycheck for taxes. Most employees pay federal and state income taxes, as well as other taxes. You won't have to pay any federal income taxes unless you make over a certain amount of money. In 2018, that amount was $12,000. When tax season comes, you will file an income tax return. Most people use a form called the 1040. You may find that you paid too much in taxes and will be getting money back or that you haven't paid enough and owe the government money. Sometimes, you'll break even. Some people choose to have more taxes taken out of their paychecks so their tax returns are bigger, while others prefer a higher paycheck and lower return. You will have to decide what's right for you.

Keep in mind that if you spend more than you have in your checking account, your account will be overdrawn. Banks charge fees for this, and they can cost you a lot of money. Eighteen-year-old Erin Walker opened her first bank account with a large national bank in California. According to an article in *Consumer Reports*, she was charged $506 in fees for an overdraft of about $120. Banks typically charge $30 to $35 each time an overdraft occurs. They do this even for very small purchases that send your account into negative territory, such as a $4 drink at Starbucks. This is why you need to keep close track of your checking account balance.

While a checking account gives you fast access to your money, it typically does not pay interest. You may also want to open a savings account. Many, if not all, savings accounts pay interest. Each month, the bank calculates the interest and provides a statement. Interest rates on savings accounts have been low in recent years. However, the money is safe and out of danger of being spent.

Another Card to Add to Your Wallet

Once you have proved to yourself and your parents that you can use a debit card responsibly, you may be ready for a credit card. If you are under eighteen, you will need a parent as a cosigner. This means your parent will be liable for your credit card debt if you can't pay.

A credit card is not the same thing as a debit card, and the two shouldn't be used in the same way. A debit card acts like cash, so it is useful for everyday purchases, such as clothing and food. A credit card is for larger items or emergencies. For example, your car may break down and need a tow and a repair. You may not have several hundred dollars in your checking account. In this scenario, using a credit card gives you some time to find the money to pay the bill.

It is very important to pay your credit card bill promptly. Many teens get credit cards with high interest rates. Banks give you the option of paying your credit card balance in full or paying a minimum amount, usually $25. Paying the full bill avoids costly finance charges and ensures that you don't accumulate more debt. This will also help you build a good credit history which is important and will be considered in some situations you may encounter later on, like applying for an apartment.

Is This Legal?

Before you accept a job, make sure what you are doing is legal. There are specific US Department of Labor (DOL) regulations regarding teen employment.

The DOL's website has an entire section devoted to youth and labor and has a lot of helpful information for young workers. For example, fourteen- and fifteen-year-olds have strict limits on the total number of hours per day and per week that they can work. Federal laws allow employers to pay a youth minimum wage, which may be significantly less than the regular minimum wage. Always check to see that you are working at your job legally.

Keep Going

Setting up bank accounts and paying taxes can be confusing. You may be tempted to let your parents or an accountant take care of your finances for you. However, figuring out your financial responsibilities can be empowering. You may make mistakes, but there are many resources available to help you. Take advantage of online tutorials and helpful phone numbers from your bank and the federal government. You will be making a huge investment in your future financial independence.

The Road Ahead

After spending some time working with kids, you may be ready to decide if this is the path for you. With some experience under your belt, you are much more valuable to potential employers. You've gotten a taste of the real work world, so use that to your advantage! Don't be afraid to sell your strengths and take pride in what you've accomplished thus far. Depending on what job you decide to pursue, you may need to go back to school. Don't let that deter you, though. Although school can be difficult and stressful, your classes will be relevant to what you want to do so you will probably find them interesting.

Of course, they'll also further your career and put you right where you need to be to get the job of your dreams. Whether you go back to school or not, getting a job can take time. But with hard work, dedication, and commitment, you'll find the perfect fit.

According to a report from the 2015–2016 school year, 57 percent of public school teachers had a master's, education specialist, or doctorate degree.

The Future

Has working with kids become a possible long-term career choice? If so, you might want to spend some time exploring career options working with children. There are incredible opportunities in the business, nonprofit, and educational communities. Reflecting on your experiences might help clarify your strengths and areas of interest. This will give you a head start in finding a rewarding career that you truly enjoy. The following are some career possibilities.

The Little Ones

There will always be a need for workers at daycare centers and preschools. While some education and training is needed, many of these positions

Make sure you know your state's laws. For example, in New York, day cares that operate more than three hours a day and supervise three or more kids must have a license or registration certificate.

do not require college degrees. Daycare providers sometimes work out of their own homes and often in larger centers. Preschool teachers can work in independently owned, nonprofit, or nationally franchised schools. Different schools require different credentials.

Some schools may expect a college degree with a focus in education, while others will accept a high school diploma. Nearly all schools require some type of training and field experience, which is either completed before your start date or, in some cases, alongside your job. State teaching certificates are generally not required. Unlike elementary schools, many of these schools follow a year-round schedule to accommodate working parents.

Teaching young children basic skills is fun and rewarding. However, it is important to note that the pay is often lower than that of teachers with professional degrees.

Why Not Start Now?

There's no time like the present! You can start preparing now for a future working with children. Many high schools offer elective classes in child development. Some schools have also added a bit of entrepreneurial spirit to their curriculum, offering business and leadership classes. Business classes are a good choice for teens who might want to become entrepreneurs in youth-oriented businesses. They teach students the fundamentals of small business, entrepreneurship, and economic theory. The Future Business Leaders of America has active chapters in many American high schools. They plan activities designed to promote self-confidence, leadership, and business skills.

There are also several nonprofit organizations that are aimed at helping teens grow their entrepreneurial skillset and knowledge. Junior Achievement (JA) is a nonprofit organization that teaches business skills to elementary, middle, and high school students. It offers classroom lessons and extracurricular activities that involve students learning about workforce readiness, entrepreneurship, and financial literacy. Similarly, Young Entrepreneurs Academy (YEA!) is an exciting opportunity for students in grades 6–12 in which they can draft business ideas, analyze market research, practice writing business plans, meet industry experts, and even launch their own companies. With 107 JA offices and 168 YEA! communities across the country, there's bound to be one near you!

OPEN FOR BUSINESS

Wouldn't it be exciting to create your own business as an adult? Imagine being your own boss. Grow a part-time birthday party business into a thriving full-time career. Open a cooking school for young chefs or a coaching school for promising athletes. Art, music, and dance education are just some examples of things that can provide career opportunities for people with those specific talents. Although it is certainly helpful, you do not necessarily need a college degree to open a business of your own. And whatever your level of education, there are always classes you can take—even online—that will boost your knowledge and provide you with useful information.

Find Your Fit

Many recreational facilities have several potential career positions. These include managers or camp directors, who hire, train, and supervise workers such as swimming teachers or camp counselors. They may help develop new programs, manage schedules and budgets, and deal with problems or concerns of children and families. Managers often learn on the job. They earn promotions by

People in management-type positions tend to work in office settings. As you think about your career, you should also think about what kind of work environment you're looking for.

showing their supervisors that they can handle more responsibility. Though these positions have higher salaries, managers often have less direct contact with children.

When considering which job might be right for you, you need to think about the types of relationships you want to have—both with your clients and your coworkers. Do you want to be with kids daily, or would you rather be a bit more removed but still working for children? It might be helpful to think of the differences between working as a camp counselor and working in the camp admissions office as an example. Don't forget that the admissions staff works with children, too; it just looks a little different. At the end of the day, though, you both have the children's best interests in mind.

Back to the Books

If you do decide to attend college, you may find that your experience working with children can help you in many ways. To start, you can use your experience as a topic for an application essay. Colleges look for students who can show that they have the maturity and motivation to be successful. In your essay, you can highlight your growth in leadership and responsibility, as well as how you've strengthened your ability to problem-solve. Discuss particular challenges that arose when working with children. Be specific in explaining how you met and, most important, overcame those challenges.

Your time working with children might have helped you decide the type of career path you want to follow. Some teens find they prefer a particular age

With some real-world exposure to working with kids, your experiences can teach you more about yourself as you learn about the jobs you are and aren't interested in.

group. Others are drawn to special needs children. They may decide to pursue health careers or a career in special education.

Teens who commit to a bachelor's degree or higher will find opportunities in education, government, medicine, and nonprofits. In most states, K–12 public school teachers require a bachelor's degree and state certification. To earn these credentials, students take education classes and complete a certain number of hours of student teaching. They also take certification exams.

In addition to working in schools, teachers are sometimes employed at museums, zoos, and aquariums to coordinate activities for young visitors. Parks and visitors' centers often hire teachers, historians, or recreation specialists to design exhibits and plan activities for children.

Doctors, nurses, nutritionists, and other health professionals can specialize in working with children. Pediatricians and pediatric nurses are often in demand. Social workers, psychologists, and psychiatrists who treat children's mental health disorders can work in hospitals, clinics, or private practice.

You may have started working with kids because you thought it would be a fun way to spend a summer. Or maybe you thought expanding a popular babysitting business might have real moneymaking possibilities. Participating in the care and education of children can be both challenging and fun at the same time. It can provide opportunities for personal growth and financial gain. No matter how you get started, working with children can become a rich and rewarding lifetime career.

GLOSSARY

chief executive officer (CEO) The highest-ranking person in a business.

deter To discourage someone from doing something, often out of worry or fear.

down payment An initial payment made in cash at the time of purchase, with the balance to be paid later.

entrepreneur Someone who starts and organizes a business.

expense The money used for a purchase.

fixed cost An expense that does not change from time period to time period. It remains constant, even with an increase or decrease in the amount of goods or services produced.

franchise An extension of a business whereby a large company licenses its brand and products to someone in order to operate many stores while still maintaining a united image.

gratification A source of pleasure or enjoyment.

interest The charge for borrowing money or the return for lending it.

Internal Revenue Service (IRS) The US government agency responsible for tax collection and tax law enforcement.

investment The act of contributing money or time into something.

levelheaded Practical and calm.

minimum wage The lowest hourly wage employers are allowed to pay their employees according to federal law.

nonprofit An organization that is not intended to make a profit.

overdraft A deficit in a bank account caused by a person drawing more money than he or she had in the account.

profit An increase in finances.

protocol A formal process or system set in place.

reconcile To make sure one's accounts agree with bank statements.

spreadsheet A financial worksheet in which data is organized into columns.

testimonial A statement, often written, that pays tribute to someone's work.

variable cost A cost that varies or changes from time to time, so it is unpredictable.

FURTHER READING

Books

Bolles, Richard N. *What Color Is Your Parachute? 2019: A Practical Manual for Job-Hunters and Career-Changers*. New York, NY: Ten Speed Press, 2019.

Cuban, Mark, Ian McCue, and Shaan Patel. *Kid Start-Up: How YOU Can Become an Entrepreneur*. Las Vegas, NV: Matcha360 LLC, 2017.

Kanold, Timothy D. *HEART!: Fully Forming Your Professional Life as a Teacher and Leader*. Bloomington, IN: Solution Tree Press, 2017.

Kho, Jeremy. *The Millennial Roadmap to a Rich Life: The Stress Less Guide to Succeed in Your Financial Life*. Amazon Digital Services, 2017.

Kouzes, James M., and Barry Z. Posner. *The Student Leadership Challenge: Five Practices for Becoming an Exemplary Leader*. San Francisco, CA: The Leadership Challenge, 2018.

Nealon, Gary. *Notes to a Young Entrepreneur: Everything a High School Student Needs to Know About Turning an Idea Into a Successful Business*. Austin, TX: Lioncrest Publishing, 2018.

Websites

Bureau of Labor Statistics
www.bls.gov/k12
Learn about different types of jobs and the economy through fun facts, quizzes, and games.

Junior Biz
www.juniorbiz.com
Brainstorm business ideas, connect with fellow young entrepreneurs, and learn about finances.

Young Entrepreneurs Academy
www.yeausa.org
Read about teenage entrepreneurs and see if YEA! offers a business class near you.

YouthRules!
www.youthrules.gov
Stay up-to-date with state and federal labor laws, employee rights, and relevant news.

BIBLIOGRAPHY

CollegeBoard.org. "College Costs: FAQs." Retrieved March 17, 2019. https://bigfuture.collegeboard .org/pay-for-college/college-costs/college-costs -faqs.

ConsumerReports.org. "Don't Get Dinged by Overdraft Fees." June 2012. http://www .consumerreports.org/cro/magazine/2012/06 /don-t-get-dinged-by-overdraft-fees/index.htm.

Driver, Saige. "Keep It Clean: Social Media Screenings Gain in Popularity." Business News Daily. October 7, 2018. https://www .businessnewsdaily.com/2377-social-media -hiring.html.

Fritz, Joanne. "15 Unexpected Benefits of Volunteering That Will Inspire You." The Balance Small Business. July 3, 2018. https:// www.thebalancesmb.com/unexpected-benefits -of-volunteering-4132453.

Gerber, Scott. "8 Kid Entrepreneurs to Watch." CNN Money. May 27, 2011. https://money.cnn .com/galleries/2011/smallbusiness/1105/gallery .kid_entrepreneurs/index.html.

Huhman, Heather R. "If Your Employees Aren't Obsessed with Work, You're Doing Something Wrong." *Inc.* January 31, 2018. https://www.inc .com/heather-r-huhman/if-your-employees -arent-obsessed-with-work-youre-doing -something-wrong.html.

IRS. "Understanding Taxes: The Quick and Simple Way to Understand Your Taxes." Internal Revenue Service. Retrieved June 20, 2012. http://www.irs.gov/app/understandingTaxes /index.jsp.

Job-Applications.com. "Daycare Jobs." Retrieved March 17, 2019. https://www.job-applications .com/childcare-daycare-jobs/.

MarketingCharts.com. "Teen Tech Use Shapes Consumer Behavior." January 22, 2009. https:// www.marketingcharts.com/industries/media -and-entertainment-7638.

Mississippi Children's Museum. "MCM Volunteers." Retrieved March 17, 2019. https:// mschildrensmuseum.org/volunteer/mcm -volunteers/.

National Center for Education Statistics. "Back to School Statistics." Retrieved March 17, 2019. https://nces.ed.gov/fastfacts/display.asp?id=372.

National Center for Education Statistics. "Teacher Qualifications." Retrieved April 11, 2019. https://nces.ed.gov/fastfacts/display .asp?id=58.

New York State Office of Children and Family Services. "Starting a Child Care Program." Retrieved April 11, 2019. https://ocfs.ny.gov /main/childcare/starting.asp.

Petrecca, Laura. "Teen Entrepreneurs Offer Tips to Aspiring Peers." *USA Today,* May 19, 2009.

Repko, Melissa. "Meet the 20-year-old McKinney High School Dropout Who Started an Education Company." *Dallas News.* August 2017. https://www.dallasnews.com/business /technology/2017/08/07/meet-20-year-old -entrepreneur-dropped-high-school-start -education-startup.

Shahar, Sagi. "The Business of Volunteering Is Business for Millennials." *Entrepreneur.* May 10, 2018. https://www.entrepreneur.com /article/312177.

Stein, Perry. "What It's Like to Be a D.C. High School Student Interning at a Big Federal Agency." *Washington Post.* July 25, 2016. https://www .washingtonpost.com/local/education/whats-it -like-to-be-a-dc-high-school-student-interning -at-a-big-federal-agency/2016/07/25/91ea6bca -4f75-11e6-aa14-e0c1087f7583_story . html?noredirect=on&utm_term=.d2e63f0eccce.

TurboTax. "Does Everyone Need to File an Income Tax Return?" Retrieved March 17, 2019. https:// turbotax.intuit.com/tax-tips/irs-tax-return /does-everyone-need-to-file-an-income-tax -return/L7pluHkoW.

US Department of Labor. "YouthRules! Preparing the 21st Century Workforce." YouthRules!

Retrieved March 17, 2019. https://www
.youthrules.gov/.

US Small Business Administration. "Write Your
Business Plan." Retrieved March 17, 2019.
https://www.sba.gov/business-guide/plan
-your-business/write-your-business-plan.

Volunteers for Outdoor Colorado. "Youth and
Families." Retrieved March 17, 2019. https://
www.voc.org/youth-and-families.

Weiss, Geoff. "This 15-Year-Old Founder Is Raking
in Six Figures with Her Booming Babysitting
Business." *Young Entrepreneur*. February 25, 2015.
https://www.entrepreneur.com/article/243322.

Wong, Kristin. "We're All Afraid to Talk About
Money. Here's How to Break the Taboo." *New
York Times*. August 28, 2018. https://www
.nytimes.com/2018/08/28/smarter-living/how
-to-talk-about-money.html.

Wood, Bev, and Rachel Wood. *I Can Earn It: The
Make Money "How To" for Teens and Tweens*.
Charleston, SC: Booksurge Publishing, 2009.

Young Entrepreneurs Academy. "Redefining
Entrepreneurship Education in America."
Retrieved March 17, 2019. https://yeausa.org
/about/introduction/.

INDEX